GH00983785

OPENED]

The Collection of Poetic Works

OPENED BOOK:

The Collection of Poetic Works

Sheena Kerley

REFLECTION OF GRACE PUBLISHING

copyright © 2018 by Sheena Kerley

All rights reserved. No part of this publication may be reproduced, distributed or transmitted in any form or by any means, including photocopying, recording, or other electronic or mechanical methods, without the prior written permission of the publisher, except in the case of brief quotations embodied in critical reviews and certain other noncommercial uses permitted by copyright law.

Library of Congress Control Number: 2018941371

Reflection Of Grace Publishing

Houston TX/77054

www.reflectionofgrace.net

Book Design : Cover Design / Reflection Of Grace Publishing

Cover Image / Ig0rZh-FPWing

ISBN: 978-0-9992182-7-3

Foreword

It has taken me a long time to understand that Life Is. That I Am. That You Are.

Open Book: A Compilation of Poetry is a tale of life's journey filled with emotions and thoughts of people who have traveled in many different shoes during this life experience. Open Book holds in its pages poetry that expresses the struggles of defining sexual orientation, raising children, searching through religion, breakups, make-ups, sex, power struggles, love, vanity, destruction and simply being lost in self. It was created to meet you where you are and help you get past where you were. This is the second publication of this book. The integrity of the work has been maintained but there are quite a few new never-before-seen pieces in this book. I hope you enjoy reading her as much as I have enjoyed creating her.

The Dedication of Opened Book

Chapters of myself that had been closed off for years lost behind traces of tears covered with glitter—we all have those things, those days, wins and losses we pretend not to remember.

Everyone, young and old, struggles with being open or being as you're told. We try to find a balance between who we are and who we want to be, whom we are said to be, who we were, and whom we are told we should be, without ever taking the time to look at who we really are. Through this life, I saw glimpses of myself and at the time couldn't recognize it. This book is dedicated to the ones who have found it as difficult as I did to be open. To be open to themselves and their personal truth.

To be open to acceptance of the past and a large measure of control of the future.This book is for you. A compilation of poems about what people, myself included, have gone through.

A series of words, some of which were written specifically from where you are to help get you through; some will make you laugh at where you have

*been and take heed before you proceed, showing you
that it's not as complicated as it may seem.*

*This book is dedicated to the ones who wonder why
they go through so many things. The people with
mixed emotions and broken spirits. The lovers of
love who have experienced great joy blended with
tremendous pain. The book is dedicated to those of us
with labels and those of us without. Those of us who
box ourselves in, closed off, only showing enough of
ourselves not to offend in broken attempts to fit in. This
book is for you, in hopes that in these short verses of
someone else's journey to become open you will open up
to your own truth.*

Unexpected Thunder

You remind me of what was, what is, what should have been, and what could be all in one glance.

Memories and fantasies intertwine like music does with dance, afraid and excited all at the same time—butterflies'—not wanting to care but unable to stop it; not waiting to want you but unable to block it, wanting to wonder what you have to profit but my brain won't do it; my mind is not allowing my thoughts to cycle the way they normally do.

I have consciously accepted that my subconscious has no walls up with you; it's sad but fortunately true for you.

I want to rebuild my walls brick by brick with mortar and cement because I'm fluent in the language of pessimism-cloaked optimism. They think I'm a square when I'm really a prism, held captive inside myself from them. I hide, trying to figure out why not with you; why am I so transparent, so see-through? Why do I trust you?

These thoughts rumble through my mind like ships in shallow waters. I attempt to tread lightly.

Twisted Fate

Even when she's weak she is strong,
But she can't find the difference between
smiles and tears dreams and fears. Her
nights and days are intertwined, a 40–
year-old soul racing through a 14-year-old
mind.
It's too much too soon.

There is an ominous presence that lingers
in her gloom; she has yet to visit life and
has already tasted death. She went to the
boundaries of the unknown and there was
nothing I could do to help, so I watched
her weep while she slept.
Wait, I digress...

She is so bittersweet—a gift of sight to
a blind man who is still surrounded by
darkness, a gift of food to a starving child
with a terminal disease, a treacherous
blessing covered in a picture of perfection.

Even when she is strong she is weak. She
has yet to learn the difference between
future and present, curse and blessing and
safety and harm. All I know is she will find
peace in his arms.

My Vanity

The vanity in me would like to say that
my arms bring peace and speak about my
pain, my worry, my grief, but ooh, the God
in me won't let me do such things, won't
let me curse or scream. Okay, I'm lying;
sometimes I allow Satan his uprising in my
soul and I Show Out! I take pleasure in my
pride and expect to be protected from the
pain of feeling neglected by anyone.

 I admit my need to be needed, my want
to be wanted, my love of being loved, and
I flaunt my gifts from above. Ooohh, I am
loud and obnoxious and drunk and free. I
run wild and naked in the streets, then I
blame it on simply being me.

Have sex with a stranger, slap her and call
her a bitch; she my strap with the world
and proclaim, "They ain't shit!" These are
simple fantasies; my vanity is my peace
of mind that controls my inner beast,
the inability to ever completely unwind,
keeping me in a nutshell, vain and unfree.
A slew of clichés

Peace of mind comes with forgiveness and
time.
The joy of just being comes from love
without reason.

Letting go sounds easy but is almost impossible to do because the things that you've gone through have grown you, built you, shaped you and will continue to do so. Like the waves shape the beach, life's experiences shape you.

Uncontrollable people create unpredictable circumstances or even predictable ones that you choose to endure; only you can ever be sure which one it truly is.

The Beginning Of Forever

With you I saw my yesterday, planned my tomorrow and enjoyed this day. You constantly fill my being with an overwhelming effervescent spirit that calls to you, interrupting my insouciant nature because I saw something greater when I accidentally glanced at you.

I was subdued by your smile, entranced by your eyes, held captive by your words, and I tried not to but I became uninhibited as you penetrated my mind. Maybe it's just my imagination, maybe my mind lies when in you I see my demise, the undoing of me, turning me into something completely new. Is it true?

Could I be completely enthralled with
you, captivated by your core capabilities
of domesticating me, educating me
and emancipating me from my past,
mesmerized by the truth in your
fascination with my mistakes, exonerating
me from my regrets as you waited
patiently for the arrival of my flaws that
you find irresistible?

By doing so you absolved me from all
insecurities and we call that a free for all
because in you I see my tomorrow as I re-
imagined my yesterdays and wait for this
day.

That One Great Love

That one great love you wait a lifetime for,
then you let it go because it hurts too much
to hold on to. That one great love that
you realize doesn't love you, not like you
love it, not like it's supposed to, not even
attempting to grow for you.

That one great love that doesn't see what's
there for them and allows you to slip
through their fingers. As you slip through
their fingertips you're dropping pieces of
you bit by bit, anticipating the shatter.

To Fool A Woman

Your fear cloaked in the need to impress
sometimes resembles confidence, like a
spoiled child who's upset and threatening
to hold its breath.

Eluding reasoning, you pushed your
dreams on her, attempting to force her to
be who you felt she should be, attempting
to brainwash her with your infectious
weaponry, teaching her that to be captive
is to be free, showing her division while
calling it unity, convincing her put out her
own light, dumbing herself down for y...

Missing You

I know I shouldn't but I do, missing you like the night misses the moon when it's new. I can't see you but I feel you as if you never left. I miss you like I miss singing; when you disappeared my voice seems to have evaporated into thin air. You were the art of my soul, the rhythm to my blues, the bass in my tune. I feel like May without June, incomplete and inaccurate, like Kool-Aid that ain't sweet.

Missing you is not bittersweet; it's disgusting, like rancid meat, maggot-infested, the wounded flesh of an animal that moans and should be put to death yet it continues to suffer and groan and pant after days long gone. Tears and singing sad songs while walking in the rain is a pain I wish I had.

This is what happens when making a smart decision goes bad. We parted ways because I was bad for you and you were bad for me. We both made mistakes but you made more; you were so insecure because you were a whore; your temper was loud and my demeanor was weak. Now I'm missing you. My timid nature fed your inner beast.

It seems as if I had rubber suction cups on my stomach because you walked all over me, pissed on my feelings and used my thoughts to scrub your feet, but I stood still. I held you up, making sure didn't fall and you stood tall. Now I miss you. I knew that the coming soon would bring your warm water of love, pour hugs and kisses and days full of laughter. Now I'm missing you because you filled my nights with nothingness. I could get lost in your lies yet I'm missing your eyes. I left my naivety there.

The desert misses the rain yet the Sudan would not be the same if a tsunami came. It would be a beach and all the life that strived there would cease. Pain vs. emptiness is the struggle you leave but I can't help but wonder if you're missing me.

Passionate Past

You—the feel of you, the thrill of you, the indecency of the things we used to do. The indulgent acts of passion that most can't even imagine, with climaxes on mountains never reaching valleys. I used to crave you so badly, so much deeper than skin to skin.

As free as Adam and Eve before they knew sin, we exceeded expectations and experienced freedom at its finest. Like salt to the ocean, you flowed through me, creating waves and forming peninsulas from sand, shakes leaving open orifices like doors with no hinges, extremities extended, living fantasies with no limits.

I became your imagination, gave you continuous incubation and you grew in me, knowing me like no other, my friend my lover, my past passion... Remember when.

Good Morning

Ready to say good morning, my king and queen, whatever you deem necessary. Dammit, I'm just ready to say good morning again. Trying not to become impatient and let destruction back in, ripping apart hearts like paper-mâché in the whirlwind of twisters I suffer day by day.

Good morning that leads to good mornings followed by cozy afternoons, entertaining days and adventurous nights. Good mornings even after horrible fights. And tense disagreements. And days where nothing goes right.

Good morning with glorious gazes and adequate rest, followed by fresh out of the shower sex, loving the way we mesh. Know that 'good morning' from you prepares me for the day's tests, and it calms me when yesterday's stress attempts to cloud my mind. If I wake up on the wrong side of the bed you reset the alarm and tell me good morning one more time.

Good morning leading to peaceful days in a lazy haze, morning glory wake and bake on rainy days, looking at the waterfall onto the beach, knowing how blessed we are to see this. No need to speak; your eyes say good morning and your smile says you watched me sleep. We don't always breath in one accord, but today you are one with me.So I gently kiss you good morning as your arms hold me, providing the energy I need for my day after a loud silent good morning filled with kisses and glowing faces.

You text me and say good morning, by the way. I walk across the room and your vibe says I miss you; when I turn the corner to the kitchen I'm saddened because I'm no longer with you. I can't wait to say good morning. I'm ready to mean it again.

Glide

I know what to do with it; sometimes I sit
and reminisce about days gone by, about
cold days and hot nights being warm by
your side. As you gaze at my fingertips
resting on my thigh you didn't realize I was
watching—I caught you from the corner of
my eye, so I play the piano gently between
my knees, pretending that I think you're
asleep.

You began to squirm and cuddle closer to
me. I felt your hand gently guide mine,
perfectly strong, not forceful; you moved
steadily and took your time. Before you
knew it your lips embraced mine and you
lost control.
 AndI know what to do with it. You still get
wet at the thought of me in it.

No need to say it; it shows when you can
sit with your legs uncrossed and your
lip gloss becomes a meal and I hear the
tapping of your heels when I come near
because six months later your legs still
shake at the thought of me. It's flattering;
it's nice to sit and reminisce about the days
gone by.

Wet

Blow on me – desperately.
Miss me – with intensity.
Punish me with pleasure, bring me alive
with pain, increase my sanity by driving
me insane, wet me - make me rain.

Not drizzle, not sprinkle; you'll think I
pissed, not tinkled. No wet spot,
A drowning pool; you're my jester - do da
fool.
I'm your captain – salute me.
I am ocean – pollute me.
Do your best when you do me; don't kiss
me – tongue me down.
Don't be silent – please be loud.
Don't be merciful – make me beg. I wanna
scream your name when you give me head.

This Morning

Waking up in peace after sleeping through
the storm, I'm in the comfort of his arms.
Miracles are performed, rocky places made
smooth, dry places made wet, low places
made high. Freed of all regret, resistance is
down, chains are broken, walls came down,
what was lost has been found, sight has
been given after years of being blinded...

(breathe) ....yep, you guessed it. Yahweh's blessing continuously pursued me. I ran until I got tired then I surrendered all. I called his name and then He came; now I'm living life for the first time again.

I Know You

I know you; I have encountered you time and time again, in different shapes and forms you fuck all your female friends, luring them in with pseudo-love and laughter. Heartache, despair, distress—these are the residues the morning after.

I am not falling for that shit again; with your poetic phrases and breathtaking gazes, you tell truths that are blanket statements sprinkled with individualized lies while looking dead into their eyes, telling them you see their soul knowing you're staring at your reflection. So you've won; she has been infected with affection for you, longing to cater to you as they all do.

You'll feed her fairytales and sell her dreams and she will unknowingly become part of a team, thinking that one day she will be co-owner because that's the part of the dream you sold her. See, I told you, Nigga, I know you—your scent, your smile, your approach, and your style. The player is now the teacher and she doesn't need a coach.

Excuses Of A Man

Life is full of the unexpected; people running around unprotected with open hearts and closed minds. My leader is in search of a leader; anyone will do, even me, even you. They would gladly follow the blind because they think it's better than nothing.

When they have no leader they feel stagnant and frail, too afraid to try because they are too afraid to fail. My protector is not scared of death yet terrified of life, doesn't know how to have a party without having a physical conflict, finding it easier to take a life than lose a fight. The provider is hanging out all night calling it chasing paper, while he is actually bringing mothers' nightmares to life.

 The breeder states I love you so much I want you to carry my seed but don't expect to be my wife; famous phrase:

"I can't commit cause I don't know how to love; no one ever taught me. I didn't have a father so I don't know how to be a man. I don't know how to work. If you love me you'll teach me how to stand. I can't teach my son because no one taught me but I can't wait to teach my lil nigga how to be a G."

3/9

Like three plus nine you're way past ten. Sometimes I sit and reminisce, wondering when I'll see you again, wanting to bury my face in your chest in hope that I'll find rest, wondering if in your presence I'll find relief from my stress, from the need to impress the masses wanting to just be. But there is too much between us, too much of you and too much of me.

So close yet so far away— you're like a daydream. It seems as if we are forever passing, revisiting this eternal affair, trying not to come when you call but the essence of me is there and the thought of you is here. When people are around they can feel it in the air; I know it because I see them looking around, trying to see who it belongs to, searching for auras or symbols of couples in love but they will look and

never find what we claimed to have let go.
There is so much between us.

Nine years and three tries never could cut
the ties. Four children – one for me, three
times it should've been mine and for nine
years my one has wanted to be yours but
you and I never could get on one accord.
You think I don't pay attention and I think
you don't care; truth is, neither one of us
is right. We just never realized it until the
end.

According to the stars we are soul mates.
But seeing that we are both strong-minded
individuals we believe in creating our own
fate. You know the mind frame: it's better
never than late because we have schedules
and things to do, plus my guard is up and I
know you too well to trust you.

I'll just be something fun to do. I'm
confident and cocky yet my insecurities
find comfort and they cling to you.
Insecurities or intuition, I don't know
which one it is, but I know that I always get
tingly at the thought of you.

You think I'm not attentive because I
don't know times and dates but I know so
much more, like your meticulous nature
and suspicions and you long for forever

with someone strong yet submissive.
When you're involved emotionally you
have a hard time getting your words out
appropriately. You're silly when you're
nervous. These things didn't just occur to
me.

Butterflies

You remind me of what was, what is, what
should have been and what could be, all in
one glance.
Memories and fantasies intertwine like
music does with dance, afraid and excited
all at the same time—"butterflies".

Not wanting to care but unable to stop
it, not wanting to want you but unable
to block it, wanting to wonder what you
have to profit but my brain won't do it. My
mind is not allowing my thoughts to cycle
like they normally do. I have consciously
accepted that my subconscious has no
walls up with you, sad but fortunately true
for you.

I want to rebuild my walls brick by brick
with mortar and cement because I'm fluid
in the language of pessimism cloaked in
optimism. They think I'm a square when

I am truly a prism held captive like a
prisoner inside myself. From the rest I
hide, trying to understand why I don't with
you, why for you I am transparent, I'm see-
through.

Why do I trust you?
These thoughts rumble through my psyche
like a ship in still waters I tread lightly.

I Hate TeeTee

From her brown eyes to the truth in her
lies,
I hate her with every fiber of my being;
from the day we met even after sex, I
detest her.
Her ability to see through me and call me
out on my mess, causing me to regret all
the nights that I stressed without her; like
an empty shell on the beach she found me
and boiled me hot, like the pot her love
overflowed.

Becoming my friend, my love, I've watched
her grow.
She is the waves that I love to dive in, with
deep blues and white foam; she is the full
moon that I wait on for manifestations
of the deepest meditations of my soul;

she is the rainbow after thc storm, the
sand to my beach, the wick to the candle
I use to pray; in my school of life she is an
unexpected snow day.

I hate her for all that she is, her inability
stay. She arrives to say goodbye and
quickly whisks away. She leaves behind
still waters hitting hard rocks and bare
skies. Piles of wax that have no light
ridiculing the blind by offering the
opportunity of sight, leaving me to stumble
in the dark and slip on black ice. I hate her.

She is the void that she fills; this explains
the void that she feels when she leaves.
I hate TeeTee because she knows how to
love me. I hate her understanding, her sex
I detest, I loathe the comfort she found
when she slept upon my breast.

It's embarrassing that I believed the lies of
forever, the implied concern as she stared
into my eyes and kissed upon my thighs.
It makes life easier to make it known
to myself and to my TeeTee that I hate
her, unwilling to entertain her presence,
reluctant to allow her into my heart
because she pulls it apart.

Because she is the sunrise and I am the
night. I am the earth and she is the sky. I
hate her because we have yet to learn to
say goodbye.

I Loved Once

I loved once many years ago.
I loved hard and strong and it was easy,
Loving like I loved felt like being carried
on the wind.
Sometimes it was the winds of a storm;
sometimes it was the sweet summer
breeze.

I had sunshine on a cloudy day;
If you only knew took my breath away
And music soul child called us to love and
Mya sang about yesterday.

He gave me a list of things good girls don't
do,
He taught me how to ride and drive
And how when things were tough to see
them through.
He gave me swag and shared his style with
me; he made my youth fun

And for greatness, he pushed me.

He didn't like school but made sure I went. Sometimes he ran wild and left me behind but I knew that deep down in his heart, love would always be mine.

Love made me angry and made me cry; love sent my emotions on a rollercoaster ride.

In a lot of ways love has made me who I am, the good and the bad, the happy and the sad, the ups and the downs, even when love left, it was always around.

I hurt love and love hurt me back but sometimes me and love got a little carried away with that.

You know it's love when thinking about the pain makes you laugh and thinking about the tears that love made you shed makes you smile.

Love may have been late or not on point but love never completely let you down.

When I look at love on paper with a list of pros and cons alongside the others that wish to be my lover, love would lose hands down except for the one pro on love's paper.

I loved once and I will never love another like I love because

Love captured my soul and enchanted my heart; love is intoxicating and is a work of

art that can never be duplicated. I loved
love so much that I am infatuated.
And trust me, honey, it's not just a rhyme.
Sometimes I wish it were, because if you
know like I know love hurts; that's why I
only loved once And I haven't stopped yet
because I don't know how.

Love locked me in a maze; I have yet
to find a way out. When love calls me I
always come running. Even if I'm hesitant,
sometimes I make love wait like love does
me. You see, we play this game of hide
and seek. When love is ready I am not and
when I am ready love has moved on. It's
time for this game to stop. I need love to
come and stay home.

Signed, humbled and forgiving.

Crown And Coke

Crown and Coke in a short glass, light ice.
This is the first time I've ordered this
drink for myself but the words rolled off
my tongue like they'd been there for years.
I think this is my new drink, for the rest of
my life.
Change is inevitable; to forgive is divine.

There is nothing new under the sun. So the chain of changes that started in me and ends in you inevitably increased my want too. I mean I want you. I mean I wanted you even when I didn't want to and now I need you. I need you to sit and view thousands of sublime, individualized, never-seen-before sunrises with me.

This is the part of me you thought you'd never see, or so you say because that can't be. Your resiliency shows me either insanity or you knew subconsciously that you could pull this side out of me. You believed in me; you saw me when I couldn't see myself when I saw average you saw amazing.

Now I'm sitting here drinking Crown and Coke with light ice, hoping I found something new under the moon, that this experience is completely new, that I continue to love the redundancy of watching the sunrise with you because even in its repetitive nature, I'm guaranteed something beautiful and something new.

The End Of An Era

The end of an era, the beginnings of
a nation—our seed shall sow the seed
that will improve the universal rotation.
Because I am drawn to you, can't pull away
even if I wanted to.

I'm connected to you in ways I don't
understand. You make me grateful to be
a woman simply because you are a man. I
hope you realize what you have awakened
in me.

He Kissed Me

When I told him about you, he kissed
me and reassured me that he was excited
about you. You set off a flame in him that
I could not do alone or so quickly. Before
you were in outward existence he was in
love with you, like he'd known you for
years.

My son, my prince, he was the king in
you before he heard your heartbeat. He
admired you before you were proven true.
You are loved.

This Place Again

Getting here is a mystery.
I know I've been to this place but it all
seems foreign to me. Everything changed
about me.
Sure, I made mistakes along the way but
sometimes I can at least pretend to be
human, right? Do I have to be superwoman
all the time? They say to err is human, to
forgive is divine.

Well, I should be mush white candy
from all the forgiveness I've passed out
in the short 29 years of my life, gifting
forgiveness through fear and tears. So oh
lord, here we go, we gon' try this one more
time. But how? How did I get here this
time?

Instinctive

Follow my first mind.
Complete my thought.
 Finish my sentence.
Accept my repentance and ignore yours.
It's instinctive, isn't it—the things we do
and the lack thereof, all for the sake of
love.

The amount of us and the lack of I, like seeing the storm clouds in a distant sky, seeing love when you close your eyes, ignoring the signs, refusing to realize, pretending not to know that you have intuition into the unknown, instinctively approaching the dark, not afraid to go alone for the sake of what it could be if... If it's not what it should be, excited about what it may become because the smell of the rain excites me when I see the storm approaching.

A Crown

An addiction to Crown and Coke left me lost and alone with an old friend that I lost in my binge.

Something Forgotten

Wait just one second; see, you were going so fast toward your task I think you might have left me. I'm glad I caught you. I'm surprised you stopped. I've called to you numerous times.

You glanced and gave a nod, not even a
moment's time. You had some people with
you when you knew me well, the ones you
said you'd never lose—you know those
good ones who picked you up when you
fell,
the ones that love you, that helped you get
on your feet. I guess you …

She Sends Me

Destiny sends me on journeys for
countless miles filled with second
guesses and certain smiles. Endless days
when knights don't come—one of the
most beautiful conundrums I have ever
happened upon, regretless kisses and
endless gazes cast by hearts and eyes,
trapped in mazes, late days filled with
lustful hazes and prideful phases ending in
sweet romances.

The pictures fell as waterfalls rained and
from that moment on my destiny changed.

The Broken

When I remembered you, I forgot about
me, wondered if I had ever truly been
complete. Was my boss bitch confidence
honestly a facade of constant competition
with myself? Trying to become a better
me, day by day by day, always trying to be
better than I was yesterday as if to say I
want to be better tomorrow because I'm
not good enough today.

Revisiting every single mistake, second-
guessing every decision, fantasizing
alternate endings, moving forward and
calling it forgiving but housing resentment
somewhere deep down in me that would
only reveal itself when I was alone at night
and no-one was around to see me cry, as
the heart of me dies; but my bank account
was all right, my family was fed, and bills
were paid, never having a problem getting
laid, then I remembered you while walking
alone in the rain and it felt like I walked
through the volcanic High Cascade.

How long had I lived a life that way and thought it was okay? And then I remembered you, and I saw the me you saw in me and forgot about the me that I had become, always trying to be someone else's number one. Sometimes the well-put-together are genuinely the broken ones.

True Black

If True black is you then tell me your name.
Tell me of the place from which your ancestors came.
Tell me if True black is the absence of all color.
Tell me, if they call you nigger, does that make you my brother?

Tell me why you hate who you are, or is it that you hate what you have become?
Tell me, if his skin is lighter, does that make him less black than the darker ones?
Tell me if you truly care if I put weave in my hair, contacts in my eyes and try my best to stay out of the darkening lights.

Tell me why you love it when I do those things; tell me why that makes you drawn to me.

Is this why you called me a real down bitch
instead of a real true queen?
Is this why I am your gal and not your wife
biblically?
If I say I am true black, does that make me
a liar?
If one of my forefathers happened to be a
slave owner what does that make of me,
since I heard you say that true black can't
be light like me?

Now Breathe

Breathe insight into me, rushing through
my blood flow, creating a clean heart in
me.
Breathe love into me, enabling me to
forgive myself for the things I've done
intentionally against your will, seeking
thrills and vengeance, lashing out in
haphazard rage.

Never genuinely forgiving, never turning
the page, just ripping it out and throwing
people away because they didn't behave
as I felt they should even if it was due to
being misunderstood. Breathe the breath
that allows me to love me for all that I'm
not while accepting all that I am that I
cannot change, remaining whole even
through the pain.

Breathe strength into me so that I can experience the patience in love and the kindness to the unkind, the longsuffering of the blind and understand their perception of time is not always on the same clock as mine. I need strength to strive for better than yesterday with doing more than getting through today.

Truth is what is.
Truth is what has been.
Truth is what will be.

He Lives In Me

He survives in my smile and shows himself in my stride. I abide in Him and He in me. When I've strayed too far away, my soul gets weak, and the need to be in his presence pulls at me and forces me to my knees.
And I Am is there, and I am grateful to be there. He always meets me there. He sees me there and allows me to be bare.

Realizing that I have always been well-put-together even when I feel as broken as I do, I guess this time I was hoping that maybe it would be...

Sufficiently me, making smart decisions, refusing to let my outward condition reflect my inner indecision. Permitting myself to write my ending using a pen that's Yahweh-given.

Enabling myself to complete my missions with no intermission, withholding no forgiveness, while allowing no provisions for passengers with lackadaisical natures. All steps are calculated, only taking those who can keep up with it.

One Time

Once I was running, then I stood still. Once I wondered what they were saying, then I started to spit. Once I would only spit hot shit that made the crowd quiver, then I started spitting words that got the crowd delivered.

Once I was arrogant, then I found peace, peace without sacrificing ambition, gaining a relationship and losing religion, perseverance through prayer no longer through pain. Accepted who I am and embraced my change.

When you wake up, and it's hard to move,

move anyway. When you're tired of stressing about taking the next step, stop stressing and take a step in the direction of God. When you feel like you have no choice, don't make one just prayer and be still for a moment with God. Just hold on; He hasn't failed you yet because you're still here. We make our biggest mistakes when we act without consulting God first. I am.

Thank You

I'm so grateful for every hard time that you brought me through,
For the rainy days that made me grow, for the times I almost drowned when I learned to stop panicking and think.

I'm so grateful to the people who walked away from me, left me, even used me—you were an answer to prayer and a lesson learned.

Grateful for my aches and pains because they remind me to feel, for late nights thinking with an overactive mind, for hitting my funny bone and stumping my toe, for th...

Inspire

Inspire me, love me with insanity, pamper me provide me with gravity by reminding me of how beautiful the ground is in ways that improve my reality, reminding me that from the dust we came from and to the dust we will return, that the sun does so much more than burn.

Remind me where home is, that we don't have to keep up with the Joneses; we are the Joneses. Speak to me, gracefully handle me with care, remember that it is not your job to remind me that life isn't fair.

If you love, provide and protect, I will vow to submit, respect, and take care of you, like no other granting wish like a genie, pouring myself into you until we will be become one, never stopping, never being done.

Of all the men at the city gates, they would envy you. I will help you create a life that will make your father proud, and your mother too.

But you must love me with insanity, and to do that, you must know what that means.

Blessed

A labor of love to preserve, life to do what is best for someone without having to think twice.

To give without receiving, to believe without seeing, to ensure your life has meaning that is long-lasting for someone else is the most significant gift to yourself; to be selfless and yet accept blessings without expecting,

because God knows that blessing a selfless person is blessing not just them but everyone near and far from them.

Giving yourself to others is your greatest gift to HIM. Live life without fear, know that death is a step in life. Would you give your life to save a stranger, would you accept an abandoned child into your life?

Would you be a blessing with your last, could you forgive a rapist his past, would you clothe your worst enemy knowing the wrongs he'd done you? Can you smile through adversity and take no praises, accept no glory, giving all the credit to HE who died for you? Would you let a weeping mother cry to you in the midst of your family madness? Would you speak for the wrongly accused and give your voice to those who have none, risking persecution?

Simply put, would you do what was done for you or is his love one-sided and not paid forward? While you enjoy your blessings today, make sure you answer true and be sure to do for strangers what Yahweh has done for you.

Hours Time

I spent an hour with God today, and nobody knew it. Nobody but me and Him sharing our most intimate thoughts, giving all of ourselves to one another. I gave until I was empty and he poured out until he filled me and I overflowed.

Contentedly I sat in the dark silence, listening as he spoke boldly to me and my light was bright again.
Yes me, the one who is full of sin, judged by people because of what they see, not understanding why I receive my blessings. My father deals with me privately, no need to show the world for me. This I know to be true: my father loves me.

He may not like all that I do, yet He knows my heart is true. He gives to me because even though you despise me, I give freely unto you. I could go in on the sin within the saints but I won't. Because I just gave an hour to my father, and he wrapped his arms around me.

Oh, how I've missed him so, as of late my prayers were brief and on the go. He missed the alone time with my soul. When messages didn't relieve my tension, my posture became tense, my hair just won't act right, and words don't make sense; when my smile wouldn't come back right, and my house wasn't a home, I knew it was something, but I couldn't pinpoint what was wrong.

I spent an hour with my father and prayed and smiled. I listened and talked, an exclusive conversation between father and child.

Where The Good Girls Are

A man asked me why she became androgynous, with a dark fear of deep penetration, bearing hips that could build nations draped in men's attire and saggy jeans.
I stated, "That's just what she prefers."

A woman asked me if I knew how the androgynous one could shield her beauty and deal with the lack of affirmation from the other sex, and why she would hide her cleavage and this lady just couldn't believe it, how she awoke with such natural beauty and no need for confirmation from a woman or a man.
I answered, "Confidence and self-esteem to the extreme."

A child asks no questions, only observed, looked up to her mother and said, "Why don't you smile like her?" The lady in her stilettos, bustier, and a blazer holding her humongous purse looked at her daughter and spoke with seriousness in her tone. "She is smiling because she is confused, awaiting a husband to define her and diffuse her insanity.

Remember, you are a woman; you beauty is supposed to hurt. Happiness is not first or second. You must be a good girl or Mommy's heart will burst." Then she stood silent, remembering when that was her, the androgynous one.

Hindsight

I fell in love with you in one night,
Gave myself to you, and all the crevices of
my body were malleable to your whims.
Every moral and standard that I hold so
dear went out the window when I created
an inborn fear: What if? What if I never
see him again? What if I don't wake up
tomorrow? What if I do and he doesn't?
What if another has his heart?

Not being able to bear these thoughts I
had no perplexing ideas requiring deep
contemplation; I had no internal fight. I
gave you all of me at once, for my love at
first sight.

I pulled you under the covers and kept you
there for three days' time. I kissed you and
smothered you with all the parts that once
were mine; with all of my strength, I made
you weak, ensuring that your pores reeked
of me.
 I left no mystery about the innocence
of me for you to hold onto. I held back
nothing and covered no holes full of
transparency, straight through my soul.

Your smell intoxicated me; inoculated
by your taste, your touch rendered me
speechless, having visions with no sight,

the sound of your breath resonates in my
bones. If you had called I would have run
to you at light speed; you were my desire.
But you didn't see; in three days you rose.

I wish I could say you ascended and
raptured me to heaven to hold me in
blissful eternity. I cried for weeks; I was
non-existent. You could see me and not
speak, so incomplete. We still reek of
the stench of spoiled assurance on our
essence. You emptied me, and I still see
you in my sleep.

The Forgotten

What happened to family and legacy and
pride in where we came from, ownership
of something to leave with your loved
ones?
When did prayer become a task? How can
you live if you move too fast for GOD?
What happened to love that stood against
the odds?

My grandma told me a promise used
to mean something, a handshake was a
contract and because you were black, black
would always have your back. How did top
priority get from family to financial gain?

We have become so superficial we equate
success with pain and loneliness to growth.

No there are no oaths that hold true. Oh,
oh Hebrews, where have we lost you? We
have lost ourselves and tried to play catch
up with society trying to obtain all the
things that my slave owners denied me but
lost everything that Yahweh had Provided
me.

I used to be resilient; now I am a weak,
an easily broken and partially uprooted
tree. My men are lazy, my women no
longer know their place, the children
raise themselves, we eat take out and use
paper plates, soul food is sold in chains by
people with no soul, we leave our babies at
daycare, and our old are in homes.

What happened to my people? I long to
rescue you and teach you again to know
right from wrong, good from bad, blessings
from vanity and peace from insanity.
I wanna show you how to pray again and
how to sing those old hymns, how to talk
to Yahweh and respect the earth, how to
build machines out of dirt and keep them,
how to raise your children not just feed
them, how to be a man and a woman too.
The problem is I think I have forgotten too.

Stability

Sometimes I understand why you are the way you are, why you leave the way you leave, and sometimes I wish I could live for me the way you live for you, but I bear the weight of the thought that without me what would they do? I am only allowed pieces of peace, never an entire hour of thinking only of me. So when someone puts too much into me, I retreat.

I don't know if I feel undeserving or I feel guilty for being worthy, or I have a fear of what they will need from me, so at the sight of new things, I retreat. I'm secretly jealous of your spirit of what I imagine it is. We are tied together by being torn, for you are free and I am the weak, and I am chained and strong.

Stupid Love

If love were smart, she would give up on me. Sometimes I feel I need a master; it would be easier to follow his lead—no decisions, no choices, no worries, no woe. She is freedom and happiness and growth if you make the right choice and cast the right vote, answer the correct calls, speak

the right lines, be in the right place at the
right time. She is confusion and ruckus,
and she must learn to trust us and we her.

Amongst all the abuse I received from
her I got a contusion; she became a blur.
Sometimes I think it would be easier
without her.

A Moment Of Peace

As the wind kisses me softly, the clouds
drip their sweet nectar to the pink roses in
bloom.
The rustling of the leaves in the beautiful
trees stir the birds to sing. And oh, the
peace it brings.
A relaxing touch of nature that nurtures
you all day—the nectar of the clouds and
the song of the birds, the kiss of the breeze
are the reminiscence of God walking the
earth.

Everyone is searching for peace of heart
and peace of mind, a silver lining in
their clouds instead of enjoying the rain,
wanting everything now when all you need
to do is look around and see the beauty
in the cloud, knowing that growth comes
with rain, understanding the beauty in

death is the release from life and all its
pain. A moment of clarity during calamity,
a moment of rest, peace that passes
understanding are all inborn gifts.

Magnolia Tree

A magnolia tree may lean but it still stands
strong, still produces beautiful flowers
and gives shelter to all those that call it
home, similar to the way I find safety
in your arms. Every word is intentional;
every emotion is original. Yes, I've loved
before but not like this. How do you love a
memory and mist?

Fragrances

The scent of you calls to me, memories
trapped in the magnolia trees, lilies, and
are carried in the breeze.
The aroma of you soothes me when I'm
lost or confused,
When it hurts and I don't know why,
When I wanna break down and I refuse
to cry, when my soul is aching and I have
made a decision on who I choose to be and
the process of ripping chunks out of me is
draining me.

The fragrances of your cakes and fresh-
cut peas on the front porch push the tears
from me way down deep, Maire.

I am unsure if you would like the woman
I've become, but I'm certain that you
would love the woman I will eventually be.

 I speak inconspicuously as to preserve
the mystery of me; concerned about who
I used to be is not what you should be
because Yahweh has changed me.
No, he found me because he made me
wonderfully and beautifully and he hid
himself in the depths of me, because deep
calls unto deep so he knew that eventually,
I would have no choice but to seek, to
reach out for him, to indulge myself in his

word and every living word that he has
provided me because faith comes by—well,
you know the rest so I apologize for getting
off track.

 I forget where I was going with this, but
Yahweh, I need you back.

Always The Friend

Always the friend—now I know how he
felt, for years mocked and left behind, just
spinning wheels.
I'm always sticking myself to iffy
situations, longing for the emotionally
unavailable, unfaithful to the faithful
and grateful to the ones that neglect me
because "I'm busy."

With a heart broken time and time again
by one who wanted me first, now I'm so,
so thirsty yet afraid to drown, so I drink
dirt. Choking hurts less than drowning; it
astounds me the security I find in simply
being me.

Yes, a plus one would be nice but just
anyone's not right;
it just inhibits the embracing of a destiny
of solidarity while the strangers next to me

try to hook me up.
I'm flattered but I'll pass' like I said,
"shattered picture in broken glass." I
choose those who don't choose me so that
it's impossible to lose me in them, so I
always win. Even when I feel like I lost I
have won again.

Decent And In Order

I have always taught you that everything
should be done decently and in order.
There is no madness in the method; don't
make messes that teach you hard lessons,
every day count your blessings and don't
fool around with people that are stressing.

To My Will To Write

I'm trying to focus
I'm trying to focus here! I yell silently.
I don't wanna be a lyricist anymore; I
wanna help people win. I wanna teach
them that they already won even when it
appears as if they are farther away from
their destination than when they began, so
I don't wanna be a poet.

Sure, I can write a rhyme at the drop of
a dime that causes emotions to swell,
like the wells of eyes baring the pain of
liberation as we go through the birthing
pains of changing a nation.

Yes, words still drip from my lips that
cause real ones
to grip hips that are curved to perfection,
supporting erections with verbiage that
builds the foundation for nations to
blossom from wishing wells in hidden
places between the thighs of queens.

No, I haven't forgotten how to tell fantastic
stories about how goons got gory, faced the
courts and the jury with enough currency
to set them free.
I'm ready to teach people now that true
currency in energy, wealth can't be
attained without inner peace, the ego is

your inner beast expressed outwardly, sex without love is cowardly, GOD can't be boxed by religiosity.

I poured out my past on these pages for the purpose of entertainment, hoping that you find useful in your changes, giving insight into a confused girl's heart. Made myself an Open Book placed my secrets between the pages. I'm not going to be a poet anymore, a lyricist either., I can sing but I'm no songstress.

I will continue to be a healer. When you see me it's like walking past the wind. I see who you are; you will be one that only knew me when our paths crossed and it could have been amazing, if only you wanted to journey with me, through life's mazes, while I enjoy brushing up against every corner, nook, and cranny. I don't want to have to decide between my freedom and a family. My soulmate will be free with me, roaming the world teaching and healing, open to feeling.

With eyes only for each other, husband and wife, father and mother, karma and love are our best friends because we give without expecting and we receive with no end.

When you see me you feel the wind, and you will say I almost had her once; I knew her when.

The Beginning

Printed in Great Britain
by Amazon

59566001R00037